MW01624833

The Worship Writer's Guide

The Worship Writer's Guide

Fourteen Lyrical and Melodic
Tools for Crafting Excellent
Praise and Worship Songs

Dan McCollam

© Copyright 2012—Dan McCollam

All rights reserved. This book is protected by the copyright laws of the United States of America. This book may not be copied or reprinted for commercial gain or profit. The use of short quotations or occasional page copying for personal or group study is permitted. Permission will be granted upon request.

Published by:
iWAR (Institute of Worship Arts Resources) and
SOUNDS OF THE NATIONS
6391 Leisure Town Road, Vacaville, California 95687

Cover design by:
Paul Wayland Lee
PaulWayland Lee.com

ISBN: 978-0-9851863-2-6

Printed in the United States of America

First Edition: June 2012

Contents

INTRODUCTION

Worship songs have an amazing ability to transform the atmosphere and release the realities of heaven. All worship writers have that innate desire to capture a moment of worship that enraptures the singer into a pure God encounter. Sometimes, a great worship song like this will just hit us all at once like a sudden lightning bolt of inspiration. However, if the only way we can write a great worship song is through this sudden jolt of external inspiration, then we may tend to sit around waiting for the next thunderstorm to happen.

There is another way.

Creativity is not just inspiration; it also has its deep roots in wisdom, knowledge and understanding. *The Worship Writer's Guide* is designed to give you the song craft tools that are based on the timeless principles of great songwriting. These powerful lyrical and melodic tools will help you tap into the wisdom that births great worship songs.

The concepts in this book are set up in an easy-to-follow, quick-guide format that won't bog you down with mechanics but wil liberate your creative urge through the principles of effective communication. Each short chapter is followed with a few simple exercises that activate your understanding of each key principle.

If you have ever been to one of our training workshops, you know that we use current popular songs as examples. In this book we have chosen to use hymns for several reasons.

First of all, hymns have stood the test of time. They are enduring works of art and craftsmanship that give great examples of strong worship writing. These praise and worship songs have impacted generations of worshipers.

Secondly, most hymns are public domain and don't require written permission for use. This makes them more accessible and affordable for both the student and the teacher.

Finally, the melody and lyrics to hymns are already known and loved by many people. If you are not familiar with the melody of one of our examples, you can find it and hear it for free by searching the title of the hymn or the word "hymn" on the internet.

While hymns give us a great example of the enduring craft behind worship writing, I think you will find the principles are even easier to apply to current popular music styles. Get ready to enjoy learning the art of crafting a great worship song from the fourteen lyrical and melodic tools in *The Worship Writer's Guide.*

SECTION ONE

SEVEN LYRIC-CRAFTING TECHNIQUES

Step One	Count Syllables
Step Two	Underline Repetition
Step Three	Circle Rhymes
Step Four	Superscript Lists
Step Five	Connect Opposites
Step Six	Identify Word Palettes
Step Seven	Recognize Song Form

Step One

Count Syllables

Before you begin, please write out the lyrics to three of your favorite praise and worship songs. Make sure you save these lyric sheets so that you can use them throughout the course.

❧ ❧

Our first step to discovering what we love in any song lyric is to count the number of syllables in each line or phrase of the song. Count the syllables as they are sung, not just how they are written, since often a songwriter will assign two or more notes to a single syllable. Place the number of syllables of each line in the left-hand margin of the written lyric as in the following example:

7	O come, let us adore Him
7	O come, let us adore Him
8	O come, let us adore Hi-im
4	Chri-ist the Lord

"O Come, All Ye Faithful" by Frederick Oakeley, Public domain

Note to self: same words, different count

Notice how each of the first three lines are made up of only seven syllables, yet the last line of the three phrases is sung with eight syllables. This is because the word "Him" at the end of the third line is sung with two tied quarter notes.

The last phrase is written with only three syllables but sung as four. So the structure of this chorus would be written as 7-7-8-4, not 7-7-7-3.

Counting syllables helps you discover the balance, symmetry, and line cadence of musical sections. Each matching song section should have approximately the same syllable count. For instance, a second verse would have roughly the same word and syllable count as the first verse. Many novice writers neglect this use of balance and symmetry in their own songwriting.

Exercise: Count the Syllables

From the lyrics of the three praise and worship songs you selected, count the syllables of each line.

Song One

Song Two

Song Three

Step Two

Underline Repetition

Repetition plays a key role in writing great songs. In the songs you have selected, do you find a pattern of repetition in the verse or chorus section? Underline key words or phrases that repeat in your song list.

Here is an example:

Nothing But the Blood

<u>What can</u> wash away my sin?

<u>Nothing but the blood of Jesus</u>

<u>What can</u> make me whole again?

Nothing but the blood of Jesus
Oh precious is the flow
That makes me white as snow
No other fount I know
Nothing but the blood of Jesus

"Nothing But the Blood" by Robert Lowry, Public domain

Note to self: repetition is a good way of crafting song sections.

The composer uses a definite pattern of repetition in this hymn. Each of the A sections (or first song sections) start with a two-word phrase that is repeated in the third line. In the first section of the above song, that phrase is "What can..." Then each second and fourth line repeats the hook, "Nothing but the blood of Jesus." At the final line of the B section, the hook "Nothing but the blood of Jesus" is repeated again.

Notice that the worship writer, Robert Lowry, uses this repetition pattern for each of the A (verse) sections.

In the following exercise, underline all the examples of repetition found in the second verse of Lowry's classic hymn.

For my pardon this I see

Nothing but the blood of Jesus

For my cleansing this my plea

Nothing but the blood of Jesus

Oh precious is the flow

That makes me white as snow

No other fount I know

Nothing but the blood of Jesus

Not every song uses lyrical repetition, but many will. When lyrical repetition is found, make note of where and how it is used.

Exercise: Underline Repetition

Check for the use of repetition in the songs you have chosen. Note how often repetition is used and in what section of the song.

Step Three

Circle Rhymes

Circling rhyming words helps us to identify whether a specific rhyme scheme is used. Let's return to the lyrics of the Robert Lowry hymn as an example:

Nothing But the Blood

What can wash away my **sin?**
Nothing but the blood of Jesus
What can make me whole **again?**

Nothing but the blood of Jesus
Oh precious is the **flow**
That makes me white as **snow**
No other fount I **know**
Nothing but the blood of Jesus

"Nothing But the Blood" by Robert Lowry, Public domain

Notice that we have highlighted the last word of the first and third line because of their rhyming scheme. These are examples of "slant" and "perfect" rhymes most often used in hymns which we will be examining.

Note to self:
rhyme patterns
help me know
what I like
in a
song lyric.

Slant rhymes are words that have the same sounds but don't form a perfect rhyme. Often both slant rhymes and perfect rhymes will be used within the same song.

Regardless of whether a song uses perfect or slant rhymes, a pattern should be identifiable.

With the above chorus, circle and connect all the other words that rhyme with each other.

Now check to see if the composer uses the same rhyme scheme in the second verse:

For my pardon this I see
Nothing but the blood of Jesus

For my cleansing this my plea
Nothing but the blood of Jesus

We can see here that Robert Lowry does use the same rhyme pattern in each verse. With this information we can establish the fact that he is using rhyme intentionally in the first and third line of each A section. It is also worth noting that Lowry uses a contrasting rhyme scheme in the chorus.

Exercise: Circle Rhyming Words

With the songs you have selected, circle any rhyming words that you find. Connect the rhymes with a line and look for a rhyme scheme or pattern. Include in your search slant rhymes.

Step Four

Superscript Lists

Many popular songs use a list method of building their lyrical composition:

All For Jesus

All for Jesus! All for Jesus!
All my days and all my hours;
All for Jesus! All for Jesus!
All my days and all my hours.
Let my hands[1] perform His bidding,
Let my feet[2] run in His ways;

Let my eyes[3] see Jesus only,

Let my lips[4] speak forth His praise.

"All for Jesus" by Mary D. James and Asa Hall, 1871, Public domain

Notice the stanza is built with a list of four prayers:

1. Let my hands...
2. Let my feet...
3. Let my eyes...
4. Let my lips...

> Note to self: when composing a song, the list technique can help me craft song sections.

The list method is a very common technique for crafting the body of a song section. Repetition of a key word is a common sign that points to the use of the list method. Obviously, in this song, the phrase "Let my..." is the repetition key that helps us recognize the use of the list.

Identify the list that is used to build the stanza in the following song, "Leaning on the Everlasting Arms." When you find the list, superscript it by placing a number above the concluding word of each phrase. See the example above if the directions are still unclear.

Leaning on the Everlasting Arms

What a fellowship,①

What a joy divine,
Leaning on the everlasting arms;
What a blessedness,
What a peace is mine,
Leaning on the everlasting arms.

"Leaning on the Everlasting Arms" by Dalton, Georgia, A. J. Showalter & Company, 1887, Public domain

The writer used the following list to build his song:

1. What a fellowship
2. What a joy
3. What a blessedness
4. What a peace

Exercise: Superscript Lists

Check for the use of this list technique in the songs that you have chosen to examine .

Number the lists with superscripts.

Step Five

Connect Opposites

Another technique for crafting a song section is to use opposite words within a song phrase. Notice how the writer used opposites to build the first line of the hymn, "Just a Closer Walk with Thee."

I am **weak** but Thou art **strong**.
Jesus keep me from all wrong.
I'll be satisfied as long.
As I walk, let me walk,
Close to Thee.

"Just a Closer Walk with Thee" Arranged by Henry Smith, copyright ©1965, Gospel Publishing House

Note to self:
I can use opposites to craft song sections

Draw a line to connect the word "weak" and the word "strong."

Many song sections are built using this contrast method.

Find the contrasting words or phrases in the following verse of "Onward Christian Soldiers."

Crowns and thrones may perish,
Kingdoms rise and wane,
But the church of Jesus
Constant will remain.
Gates of hell can never
Against that church prevail;
We have Christ's own promise,
And that cannot fail

Words by Sabine Baring Gould, Music by Arthur S. Sullivan, 1871, Public domain

Exercise: Connect Opposites

Now find any contrasting lines or concepts within your chosen song lyric.

Look for opposite words or concepts to identify the use of contrast.

Connect these thoughts with a line.

Step Six

Identify Word Palettes

Sometimes, when a writer wants to communicate a thought visually, he or she will create a word palette. A word palette is formed by brainstorming a list of images that have been crafted to express a single idea.

For instance, if you were trying to convey the thought that all of creation is praising God, what images might come to your mind? Henry van Dyke gives us a great example in the second stanza of his classic hymn, "Joyful, Joyful We Adore Thee."

All Thy works with joy
Surround Thee,

Earth and heaven reflect Thy rays,
Stars and angels sing around Thee,
Center of unbroken praise.
Field and forest, vale and mountain,
Flowery meadow, flashing sea,
Singing bird and flowing fountain
Call us to rejoice in Thee.

"Joyful, Joyful, We Adore Thee" by Henry van Dyke, 1907, Public domain

Van Dyke's word palette for this stanza included items in creation that reflect praise. It might have looked like this:

- The sun's rays reflecting
- Stars singing
- Beauty of a flowery meadow
- Flashing sea
- Singing birds
- Flowing fountain

Note to self: word palettes can help craft a single song into a larger section.

Brainstorming visual images can help us craft the body of a song section. The general rule for this type of lyric crafting is "show us, don't tell us." The goal is to help the listener feel or visualize what is taking place rather than to just be informed of how the composer feels.

Exercise: Identify Word Palettes

1. Practice finding the word palette in the following hymn, "Savior, Like a Shepherd Lead Us." Write your word palette as a list in the margin next to the lyrics. (Hint: things a shepherd does.)

Savior, like a shepherd lead us
Much we need Thy tender care
In Thy pleasant pastures feed us
For our use Thy folds prepare.
We are Thine; do Thou befriend us
Be the Guardian of our way;
Keep Thy flock from sin defend us
Seek us when we go astray.

"Savior, Like a Shepherd Lead Us" by Wm. B. Bradbury, 1836. Public domain

2. Check for word palettes in the songs that you have chosen to examine. Write the palette of ideas in the margin next to your lyrics.

Step Seven

Recognize Song Form

The three major song forms are:

1. Verse-Chorus
2. AABA or Chorus-Bridge
3. AAA or Verse Only

To recognize song form, you must be able to identify what is called the song "hook." The hook is the part of the song that catches and holds the listener's attention. It is often, but not always, the title of the song. A hook is musically structured to be the most memorable part of the song.

Note to self: when looking for the song hook, check the location of the title first.

Once you have found the song hook, it is easy to recognize which of the three major song forms has been used. You will see that each song form places the hook in a different position.

Let's look at the three song forms and where each one positions the song hook.

Verse-Chorus

A Verse-Chorus song always places the hook in the chorus section. The chorus is almost always the second section of the song. Often the hook is repeated several times. If the song hook is in the second section of the song and repeated more than once in the chorus, you probably have a Verse-Chorus song form.

Here is an example:

Oh, How I Love Jesus

There is a name I love to hear
I love to sing its worth
It sounds like music in my ear
The sweetest name on earth

Oh, how I love Jesus
Oh, how I love Jesus

Oh, how I love Jesus

Because He first loved me

"Oh How I Love Jesus" by Frederick Whitfield, Public domain

AABA or Chorus-Bridge

The AABA song form puts the hook in the first section of the song. This song form has two sections. The second section builds musically like a chorus but does not contain the song hook. If the song has two sections and the hook appears in the first section, then you have probably identified an AABA or Chorus-Bridge song form.

Here is an example:

Nothing But the Blood

What can wash away my sin?

Nothing but the blood of Jesus

What can make me whole again?

Nothing but the blood of Jesus

Oh precious is the flow

That makes me white as snow

No other fount I know

Nothing but the blood of Jesus

"Nothing but the Blood" by Robert Lowry, Public domain

Though the hook "nothing but the blood" appears in both of the song sections, its main introduction and repetition appears in the first section. The first section features the hook; the second section merely mentions or "tags" the hook, therefore, this hymn could be classified as an AABA song form.

AAA or Verse Only

The AAA song form features the hook line in the first and/ or the last sentence of the song. It is most easily identified by the fact that there is only one song section musically and lyrically.

Many hymns and older worship choruses are written with a single song section. If your song has one musical section and the hook appears in the first or last line of that section, then you have definitely identified an AAA song form.

Just As I Am

Just as I am without one plea
But that Thy blood was shed for me
And that Thou bidst me
Come to Thee
O Lamb of God,
I come! I come!

Just as I am and waiting not
To rid my soul of one dark blot,
To Thee whose blood
Can cleanse each spot,
O Lamb of God,
I come! I come!

"Just as I Am" by Charlotte Ellion, Public domain

Notice that in the AAA song form, there can be multiple verses but only one song section.

Just for the record: many songs will have more than two sections. Modern songs often incorporate a bridge or pre-chorus section. These are simply variations of the same three major song forms.

Exercise: Song Form

Now identify the song form used in the songs that you are examining.

Write the song form in the top right corner of your lyric sheet. As you study your favorite songs, you should also be able to identify the song forms that you like best.

Lyrical Techniques Conclusion

This concludes our study of seven lyrical techniques. By now you should be able to identify the following elements and techniques in any song:

- Syllable count
- Repetition
- Rhyme scheme
- List technique
- Contrast and opposites
- Word palettes
- Song forms

The ability to recognize these lyrical elements will lead to writing better songs. However, songs are more than lyrics; they are also composed with notes and melodies.

Let's move on to the melodic tools that are used to craft your favorite songs.

SECTION TWO

SEVEN MELODIC TOOLS

Step One	Count Notes
Step Two	Determine Range
Step Three	Identify Motifs
Step Four	Locate Builds
Step Five	Contrast Sections
Step Six	Memorable Moments
Step Seven	Verify Prosody

Step One

Count Notes

❧ ☙

You don't have to be able to read music to understand melodic tools. If you can hear notes and count them, or sound them out on an instrument, you will be fine. You can also count the notes on a piece of sheet music without knowing how to "read music."

To begin learning the melodic tools, we want to see how many notes are used in each section of the song. Let's start with a one-section AAA song that just about everyone knows, "Amazing Grace." The notes are written above each syllable of the song for this exercise. Cross out the notes that are repeated and count the total numbers of notes used in the melody line. (Please note that D^1 is one octave higher than D.)

D G B - G B
A – ma - z - ing grace

A G E D
How sweet the sound

D G
That saved

B-G B A D^1
A wretch like me

B D^1- B D^1-B G
I once was lost

D E-G E-G D
But now I'm found

D G B-G B A G
Was blind but now I see.

"Amazing Grace" by John Newton, Public domain

There are thirty-five notes in this song, but when you delete all of the duplicate notes you should be left with just six.

Those notes are: D-G-B-A-E-D[1]

Many of the top songs will have a five-note melody or less per song section. "Amazing Grace" has just one more than the popular average with six notes.

Note to self: many popular songs have a five-note melody or less for each song section.

Exercise: Count Notes

Using the sheet music, your ear, or a musical instrument, count how many notes are in the songs you are using for these exercises. Delete the duplicates and count the notes that remain.

Step Two

Determine Melodic Range

❧ ☙

Counting notes helped us determine the total unique notes that were used in the melody of the song.

The vocal melodic range of the song measures the highest and lowest notes of the song melody. It determines how far apart those notes are from each other—the distance from the lowest to the highest pitch within the melody.

To find the range of a song, write the musical note (the letters A-G) of the lowest note on a piece of paper. For those who are new to music theory, there is no "H" note. The musical notes are A-B-C-D-E-F-G and the scale starts over after G. Also, the note F in our example song "Amazing Grace" is actually an F-sharp (written F#).

Referring back to our song, "Amazing Grace," in step one, its lowest note was D. Below is an example of how we would write out the unique notes (the alphabetical letters) up to the highest note of this song. Remember that D^1 is the octave of the lower D note.

D-E-F-G-A-B-C-D^1

Now, count the notes from the lowest to the highest. You find that the melodic range of this song is eight notes.

Note to self: the range usually goes higher in the second section of a song.

In a two-section song, the range of the second section is usually higher than the range of the first. Placing the second section in a higher range helps to climax the song and keep it interesting.

By finding the melodic range on several songs, you will often find that you not only have a favorite style, but also a favorite melodic key.

Exercise: Melodic Range

1. Now perform this test on your song to find its melodic range.
2. If the song has more than one section, identify the range of each individual section.
3. Notice whether the range of the second section is higher or lower than the first.

Step Three

Identify Motifs

A musical motif is defined as a short significant musical phrase in a composition. This musical phrase is often repeated several times throughout a song making it more memorable.

The use of a musical motif in the melody is often what gets a song "stuck in your head."

In the song "Amazing Grace," there is a definite musical motif, even though the entire song is only four musical phrases. The motif is found in the first two words of the song:

D G B-G B

A – ma - z-ing grace!

This motif is repeated in the second and fourth line of the song. Notice how these phrases are musically identical to the first five notes of the song.

D G B-G B

That saved a wretch...

D G B-G B

Was blind but now...

Note to self: musical motifs make a song memorable.

Do you see why the line, "Amazing grace" is so easy to remember? It is because the melody line is repeated throughout the entire song. This is an example of a strong use of musical motif.

Simply put, a musical motif is repeating melody lines within different parts of the song.

Remember that motifs are only short musical phrases, and are usually not whole lines.

They are most often used as repeating phrases, especially surrounding the hook or chorus of the song.

Exercise: Identifying Motifs

Identify whether or not musical motifs are found within the songs you have chosen for examination.

Step Four

Locate Builds

Now that you know how to count notes and find both the vocal range and motifs, you can easily locate melodic builds within a song.

Melodic builds are most often used in musical compositions possessing two or more song sections.

A build is often used to introduce a new song section or to feature an important phrase.

Note to self: using a build in the melody can help to introduce a new song section or important idea.

The musical build, as its name suggests, is a series of ascending notes that move us musically to a climactic moment.

Musical builds are often used in movies to build anticipation for what is about to happen to the characters. In songwriting, a musical build causes us to anticipate or take special notice of what is about to come.

In the hymn, "The Old Rugged Cross," notice how the composer builds into the chorus by raising the melody on the last line of the verse. If you know the song, sing the melody to the first verse.

The Old Rugged Cross

D E^b F E G F

On a hill far a – way

F F G $F^\#$ A G

Stood an old rug-ged cross

G A G F E^b F E^b D

The em-blem of suffering and shame

D E^b F E G F

And I love that old cross

F F G F# A G
Where the dear-est and best

G G A G F Eb1 D1 C1 Bb
For a world of lost **sin-ners was slain**

"The Old Rugged Cross" by George Bennard, Public domain 1913

In the last phrase of the verse, "...sinners was slain," the melody jumps more than an octave higher than the first note of the song. This melodic climax is the build that tells you the chorus is coming.

Exercise: Locate Builds

1. Locate the melodic build in songs that you have chosen.
2. How does the build set up the coming section?
3. What does the build moment introduce within the song?

Step Five

Contrast Sections

❧ ☙

When a composition has more than one song section, the writer will often contrast each section musically. We've already learned how the melodic range of a second section is often higher than the first. If the song range of the second section is not higher, it will usually be different from the first in some identifiable way. This is one form of contrast.

Another way that contrast is achieved is through a change of melodic rhythm or meter. Robert Lowry, who wrote "Nothing But the Blood," also composed the great Easter hymn, "Christ Arose."

Christ Arose

Low in the grave He lay,
Jesus my Savior
Waiting the coming day
Jesus my Lord
Up from the grave He arose
With a mighty triumph o'er His foes
He arose a Victor from the dark domain
And He lives forever
With His saints to reign
He arose! He arose!
Hallelujah! Christ arose!

"Christ Arose" by Robert Lowry, Public domain

Note to self: use both melodic and lyrical contrast to keep interest in a song.

In the verse section of the hymn, the writer uses only quarter (one count), half (two counts), and whole notes (four counts). In the verse section, he uses mainly eighth notes (fast half-count notes).

The contrast of melodic meter between the verse and the chorus keeps the song interesting. As is often true, the chorus section of this song is also in a higher melodic range.

There are many ways to achieve contrast in a song both melodically and lyrically. Sections can be contrasted lyrically by changing the syllable count, the rhyme scheme, or even the number of lines per section. Melodic contrast usually changes the range, melody, meter, or rhythm between differing song sections.

Most songs will use contrast in the melody, meter and lyric of the song, so observe all the ways that contrast might be used to compliment song sections.

Exercise: Contrast Sections

Identify how contrast is used within the various sections of your songs.

Step Six

Uncover Memorable Moments

So far, we have examined note count, melodic range, musical motifs, musical builds, and contrasting sections. All these elements and techniques are used to craft strong songs melodically.

Yet, sometimes your favorite part of the song is not as easily defined or detected. A favorite song can be defined by the way in which one note, phrase, or melodic line is sung or played.

I have favorite songs that earned that spot by virtue of a really nice guitar solo. None of these things are normal objective elements of songwriting, but when it comes to songwriting, who wants to be normal?

We are all looking for special and unique moments in our songs. Many of our favorite moments will be more subjective than objective. All these things being true, it is still important to uncover these more subjective elements within the music.

Here are a few places to uncover memorable moments:

- A well-placed pause
- A sustained note that gives emphasis
- An interesting chord choice
- An unexpected note
- A great harmony line
- An instrumental solo
- Unique imagery
- A clever lyrical twist
- Interesting background instrumentation
- Counterparts

I think that one of the great memorable moments in hymn writing is Horatio Spafford's classic hymn, "It is Well with My Soul." I love the part of the chorus where the soloist sings, "It is well" immediately echoed by the background singers, "It is well." Then, the whole song climaxes with all singers "...It is well, it is well, with my soul." I love the various pauses and pitches that so beautifully frame this song of lamentation. It is truly a work of art.

I encourage you to watch and listen carefully to the songs that you enjoy most to uncover memorable moments. Look for ways that you too can express your own musically memorable moments that are tastefully unique.

Exercise: Memorable Moments

From the list in this section, can you identify any memorable moments in the songs you have selected?

Step Seven

Verify Prosody

Prosody in songwriting is used to define the relationship between the music and the lyrics. In other words, does the music create the same mood that the lyric is crafted to express?

Prose (lyric) + Melody = Prosody.

Returning to the cinematic metaphor we used earlier, in a film you can usually tell by the background music what is happening in the movie even if you can't see the screen.

Why? Because the music is expressing what the actors are portraying. Make sure that your music is saying the same thing as your lyrics.

Note to self: use music to create mood.

Music sets mood. Take care to match the mood of your music to the message of the song. The hymn, "Christ Arose," wouldn't have worked well in a slow, minor key. The tone of the lyric is celebratory, so the music creates the same mood. They both agree. Yet, a minor key is perfectly appropriate for the contemplative Christmas hymn, "What Child is This?"

It is important to be intentional in the prosody between our musical and lyrical composition.

Exercise: Verify Prosody

Examine the prosody of the songs you have chosen. Does melody and lyric match in prosody? What musical elements help create the mood of the lyric?

Conclusion

Putting It All Together

Now that you know how to identify lyrical techniques and melodic tools, you can continue to learn from the songs that you like best. Musical tastes and styles can change but the techniques of successful communication and song craft remain the same.

To make the best use of what you have learned, make a regular habit of using these fourteen keys to analyze popular songs in the style and genre of your choice. One of the things you will find is that great songs are not usually thrown together; they are crafted with definite elements and techniques.

Learning songwriting craft from songs that are already popular and successful is one of the best ways to stay current in your own writing.

Applying these techniques to your own songs will help you write songs that you are happier with. Most of the crafting you have learned will take place in the re-writing and revision stage. After the main creative flow has run its course, don't be afraid to rewrite your songs.

An old songwriting quip says:

"The best songs are not written; they are rewritten."

The goal of songwriting is not just self-expression; it is also communication. To express ourselves effectively, we must learn the craft, skills, and tools behind effective communication.

Use these tools we have given you to increase your ability to communicate musically the song that is on your heart!

Keep writing. Keep listening. Keep crafting better songs.

About the Author

Dan McCollam travels internationally as a prophetic speaker and trainer. He strategizes with churches and individuals to create prophetic cultures in which everyone can hear God, activate and mobilize their prophetic words, and express their own unique prophetic diversity.

Dan has developed many resources that offer a fresh perspective on the prophetic, supernatural Kingdom life, biblical character and spiritual gifting. He is well-known as a great friend of the Holy Spirit who carries and imparts wisdom, revelation and breakthrough.

Dan serves on the teaching faculty of Bethel School of the Prophets and School of Worship in Redding, California. He is part of the Global Legacy apostolic team that oversees a growing number of churches in partnership for revival. He serves on the leadership team at his home church, The Mission, in Vacaville, California, and is a director of Deeper School of Supernatural Life also in Vacaville, California.

Sounds of the Nations and iWar

After serving as a worship leader for 20 years and releasing Kingdom worshipers locally, regionally and globally on countless mission trips to nations around the world, Dan became heart-sick over the westernization of worship in the majority of churches in which he ministered. Indigenous sounds had often been labeled sinful by church leadership. Since the sounds of every tribe and nation are heard in heaven, becoming an agent in restoring the stolen authentic expressions of worship became a driving passion, and Sounds of the Nations was born.

As director of Sounds of the Nations and the Institute for Worship Arts Resources (iWAR), Dan trains indigenous peoples to write and record worship songs using their own ethnic sounds, styles, languages and instruments.

For more resources from Dan McCollam, visit iBethel.com online store and search for "Sounds of the Nations" or "Dan McCollam." Original worship music from Sounds of the Nations is also available on iTunes.

Worship Writer's Songwriting Course

Dan McCollam
A 12-Lesson Course in MP3 Format

Worship Writers Songwriting Course is a 12-part MP3 audio teaching in a live radio show format that equips you to write great praise and worship songs.

Also included are all of the teaching notes and 30 songwriting assignments in PDF format for an interactive songwriting experience.

MP3 Download : $25.00

Worship at the Next Level
Dan McCollam

Discover a fresh breakthrough in your worship experience. Learn the keys of worshipping at:

- The level of your revelation
- The level of your warfare
- The level of your desperation

Break into a whole new place in your God encounter!

Number of CD's : 1 CD Audio: $10 MP3 Download: $4

God's Favorite Word for Praise
Dan McCollam

Many Christians express their praise and worship according to their own comfort level, preference, or religious tradition. Yet Scripture clearly identifies how God desires to be praised. This CD audio teaching explores the 7 Hebrew words for praise mentioned most often in Scripture. Each brief word study gives you a clearer picture of what it means to be the kind of worshiper God is looking for.

Far from presenting a merely religious argument, this CD imparts a healing anointing and releases a strong affirmation of God's love and joy over you.

Number of CD's : 1 CD-Audio : $10.00 MP3 Download : $4

God Vibrations

Dan McCollam

This 4-CD audio series presents a Christian perspective on the power of sound.

Genesis 1:3 says, "The Spirit of God moved upon the face of the deep." Those God vibrations were the beginning of all created things.

CD 1 - Sound Foundations **CD 2** - Destructive Power
CD 3 - Creative Power **CD 4** - Sound's Healing Influence
Number of CD's : 4 **DVD** Available $35

Living on the Right Side of the Cross

Dan McCollam

What really happened on the cross? What did Jesus mean when he shouted, "It is finished?" Are you living merely forgiven or totally free?

Dan McCollam believes the cross frees us from a primary struggle with ourselves, releasing us into a pursuit of our own destiny and the destruction of the kingdom of darkness.

Originally delivered at Graham Cooke's Permission Granted conference.

Number of CD's : 1 CD Audio: $10 MP3 Download: $4

Limitless: Living the Ascended Life

Dan McCollam

Recorded at the Graham Cooke Conference, "Limitless Possibilities," in Vacaville, California, this two-part series explores the believer's limitless inheritance in Jesus Christ.

Disc One: Enter the Land of the Limitless through an understanding of the true glory of the cross. Discover how the cross of Jesus Christ is meant for more than forgiveness but also freedom from sin and fullness of all that fills God Himself.

Disc Two: Living in the Land of the Limitless explores the key to breakthrough. Discover how to follow-through on revelations, supernatural experiences, and God encounters to expand their impact on your daily life. This teaching is loaded with practical principles and applications.

Available Options:

Number of DVD's : 2 $35.00 Number of CD's : 2 $15.00

MP3 Download : $8.00

Made in the USA
San Bernardino, CA
16 January 2018